Enchanted Garden
CROSS-STITCH

Enchanted Garden
CROSS-STITCH

20 Designs Celebrating Birds, Blossoms, and the Beauty in Our Own Backyards

GAIL BUSSI

STACKPOLE BOOKS

Essex, Connecticut
Blue Ridge Summit, Pennsylvania

STACKPOLE BOOKS

An imprint of Globe Pequot, the trade division of
The Rowman & Littlefield Publishing Group, Inc.
4501 Forbes Blvd., Ste. 200
Lanham, MD 20706
www.rowman.com

Distributed by NATIONAL BOOK NETWORK
800-462-6420

British Library Cataloguing in Publication Information available

Library of Congress Cataloging-in-Publication Data

Names: Bussi, Gail, author.
Title: Enchanted garden cross-stitch : 20 designs celebrating birds, blossoms, and the beauty in our own backyards / Gail Bussi.
Description: First edition. | Essex, Connecticut : Stackpole Books, [2023] | Summary: "20 cross-stitch designs in Gail Bussi's signature chalk art style, featuring garden flowers and wildlife, many with inspirational words of encouragement. Each project includes chart, finished photo, materials, and full instructions"— Provided by publisher.
Identifiers: LCCN 2022045319 (print) | LCCN 2022045320 (ebook) | ISBN 9780811771412 (paperback) | ISBN 9780811771429 (epub)
Subjects: LCSH: Cross-stitch—Patterns. | Gardens in art.
Classification: LCC TT778.C76 B879 2023 (print) | LCC TT778.C76 (ebook) | DDC 746.44/3—dc23/eng/20220921
LC record available at https://lccn.loc.gov/2022045319
LC ebook record available at https://lccn.loc.gov/2022045320

♾™ The paper used in this publication meets the minimum requirements of American National Standard for Information Sciences—Permanence of Paper for Printed Library Materials, ANSI/NISO Z39.48-1992.

First Edition

This book is lovingly dedicated to my late mother,
Catharine Ritchie Bussi—
a lady with true green fingers, who created
and cultivated beauty wherever she could . . .
miss you, Mom!

CONTENTS

INTRODUCTION

Designing and writing this book has been an absolute joy for me; it combines two of my favorite things—the magic of gardens and wild green places and the beauty of creating cross-stitch designs that keep them blooming forever and are a daily reminder of the blessings of the earth all around us.

I believe gardens are vitally important for our mental, physical, and spiritual well-being, particularly in these times when we can feel disconnected from nature in many ways. Nature is (and always has been) a healer and guide, and we do well to honor her and protect her as best we can, whoever we are and wherever we live.

"We all need sanctuary. We need a place where we can feel safe, one that rejuvenates and refreshes us, one where we feel nourished and loved." These wise words come from Jessi Bloom's wonderful book *Creating Sanctuary*, and I also believe we can apply them not only to gardens and gardening but also to any quiet creative pursuit—like stitching! We can step away from our busy lives for a little while and spend time nurturing our soul and heart in a gentle and creative way. I don't expect stitchers who read this book to rush out and plant gardens (that is, if you don't already have one!), but my dearest wish is that in stitching these projects, you will find some garden peace and serenity growing in your heart and spreading outward like ripples in a pond.

May we learn from, love, and nurture our earth, our gardens, and our lives every day.

Gail B

"If I had two loaves of bread, I would sell one
and buy hyacinths,
for they would feed my soul."

The Koran

BASIC INSTRUCTIONS

All the designs in this book are relatively simple and quick to stitch—within the reach of a beginning stitcher, once you have the basics down. Cross-stitch, backstitch, and French knots are the basic stitches used throughout, with a few half stitches where necessary.

I stitch my designs on evenweave or linen fabrics, because I prefer the look of the finished pieces, but many stitchers prefer to use Aida, and that is certainly possible with these designs, although you may have to change the suggested colors.

DMC floss has been used to stitch these projects; its quality is excellent and the range of colors so vast! I do like overdyed threads, which give subtle shading to stitches, but I am aware that a particular range of overdyed threads might not be available to all stitchers, and there are also cost implications. However, if you want to try different threads, go for it—the important thing is to make your stitching your own!

Other things to know:

- Two strands of embroidery floss are used for cross-stitches, while one is used for backstitch. French knots are made with one strand of floss, wrapped twice around the needle.
- You will need size 24 or 26 tapestry/cross-stitch needles to stitch these projects, as well as a pair of small, sharp embroidery scissors.
- For finishing some of the designs, you will need larger dressmaking scissors, pins, and suitable cotton sewing thread (as well as a steam iron for pressing the finished projects). A sewing machine is useful when stitching some projects (like little pillows), but it is definitely not essential, and all the projects in this book can also be finished with hand sewing.

STITCHES

Full Cross-Stitch

Cross-stitch can be worked as a counted stitch over a single square on Aida fabric (shown here) or over two threads when using an evenweave fabric. Each stitch comprises two diagonal stitches that cross in the center. They can be worked individually or in vertical and horizontal rows. Keep the stitches uniform by making sure the top stitch always crosses in the same direction, from upper left to lower right.

Half Cross-Stitch

Partial cross-stitches may be used where colors abut or along the edges of a design. For a half stitch, work one full diagonal across the square (half the cross).

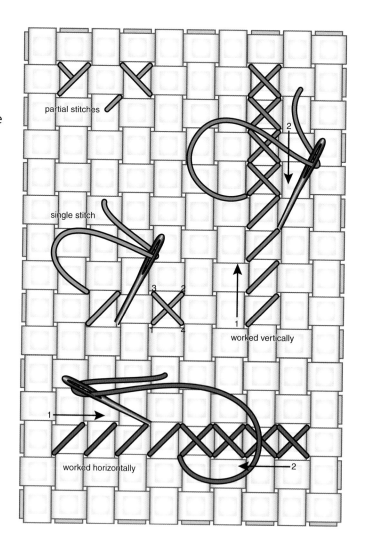

partial stitches

single stitch

worked vertically

worked horizontally

Illustrations and instructions for stitches excerpted from Embroidery Basics *by Cheryl Fall © 2013 by Stackpole Books. Used with permission.*

Backstitch

Backstitch is used to outline a shape and is worked in a motion of two steps forward and one step back. To work the stitch, bring the needle up through the fabric a stitch length's distance from the starting point and insert the needle at the starting point, working the stitch backward. Bring the needle up again a stitch length's distance from the first stitch, and continue working in this manner to the end.

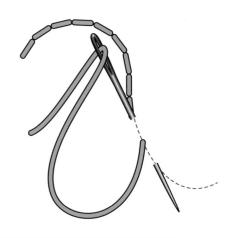

Petite Stitch

A petite stitch is a ¼-size full cross-stitch worked into one of the corners of a square.

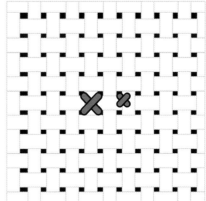

French Knot

Bring the needle up through the fabric and wrap the working thread around the needle twice. Insert the needle back into the fabric very close to (but not in) the same hole you came out of, and pull the thread through, guiding it with your opposite hand as it passes through the fabric. Do not wrap too tightly, or you'll have a difficult time pulling the needle through the knot. The thread should be against the needle, but not snug or tight. If your knot pulls through to the other side when working the stitch, try loosening the wrap a bit and make sure you're not going down into the same hole. You will need a bridge to hold the knot on the surface; usually a fiber or two in the fabric will suffice.

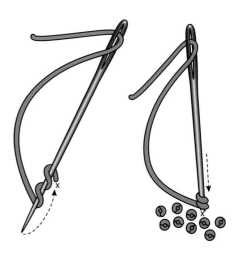

The Secret Garden

It was inevitable that this would be the first project in my book of stitched gardens, since in many ways this design, which I originally did as an artwork some time ago, was the actual inspiration for the book!

The Secret Garden, written by the American writer Frances Hodgson Burnett, was first published in 1911 and has stayed continually in print since then. Although billed as a children's book, I think it has enormous appeal for adults as well, for the story speaks to us all, at every age. On the face of it, it's a simple story of a rather plain and lonely girl who discovers an abandoned garden in the grounds of the grand house where she is living after the deaths of both her parents in India. However, the story goes much deeper than that: it's a tale of personal redemption and the importance of friendship and the natural world to us all.

There are so many lovely quotes in this book (and you will find another one used on a design later on!), but this one seemed to me to sum up how we can all bloom, thrive, and find new joy, even in apparently painful and difficult times.

"The sun is shining. That is the Magic.
The flowers are growing—the roots are stirring.
That is the Magic.
Being alive is the Magic."

The Secret Garden

Fabric: 28-count antique white Jobelan by Wichelt (stitched over 2 threads)
Stitch count: 65 wide x 137 high
Stitched size: 4½ x 9¾ in. (11.8 x 24.8 cm)

Cut the fabric, allowing at least an extra 4 inches (10.2 cm) all around, and then fold in half and count out to start stitching at a suitable point. When stitching is complete, wash the stitching (if necessary) and press with a steam iron on the wrong side. Trim the fabric, allowing at least 2 inches (5.1 cm) from the stitching on the sides and bottom, along with 3 inches (7.6 cm) at the top (to allow for the fold-over). Stitch a small hem all around, using a matching cotton thread. Fold the top down and place it over a small wooden hanger, catching it in place at the side.

Use a narrow length of satin ribbon or lace to create a hanging loop for the piece. You can also add beads or additional decorations such as small tassels or charms.

Floss Used for Full Stitches:

Symbol		Strands	Type	Number	Color
	I	2	DMC	152	Shell Pink-MD LT
	)	2	DMC	223	Shell Pink-LT
	o	2	DMC	316	Antique Mauve-MD
	3	2	DMC	353	Peach
	r	2	DMC	522	Fern Green
	L	2	DMC	524	Fern Green-VY LT
	/	2	DMC	644	Beige Gray-MD
	1	2	DMC	745	Yellow-LT Pale
	·	2	DMC	822	Beige Gray-LT
	⅂	2	DMC	928	Gray Green-VY LT
	∧	2	DMC	3012	Khaki Green-MD
	<	2	DMC	3013	Khaki Green-LT
	↑	2	DMC	3042	Antique Violet-LT
	n	2	DMC	3053	Green Gray
	c	2	DMC	3363	Pine Green-MD
	v	2	DMC	3364	Pine Green
	((	2	DMC	3727	Antique Mauve-LT
	⊗⊗	2	DMC	3790	Beige Gray-UL DK
	◆◆	2	DMC	3799	Pewter Gray-VY DK
	0	2	DMC	3855	Autumn Gold-LT
	-	2	DMC	3863	Mocha Beige-MD
	2	2	DMC	3864	Mocha Beige-LT
	~	2	DMC	3866	Mocha Brown-UL VY LT

Floss Used for French Knots:

Symbol		Strands	Type	Number	Color
	●	1	DMC	223	Shell Pink-LT
	●	1	DMC	316	Antique Mauve-MD
	●	1	DMC	3363	Pine Green-MD

Floss Used for Back Stitches:

Symbol		Strands	Type	Number	Color
	―――	1	DMC	522	Fern Green
	―――	1	DMC	3012	Khaki Green-MD
	―――	1	DMC	3363	Pine Green-MD
	―――	1	DMC	3790	Beige Gray-UL DK
	―――	1	DMC	3799	Pewter Gray-VY DK
	―――	1	DMC	3863	Mocha Beige-MD

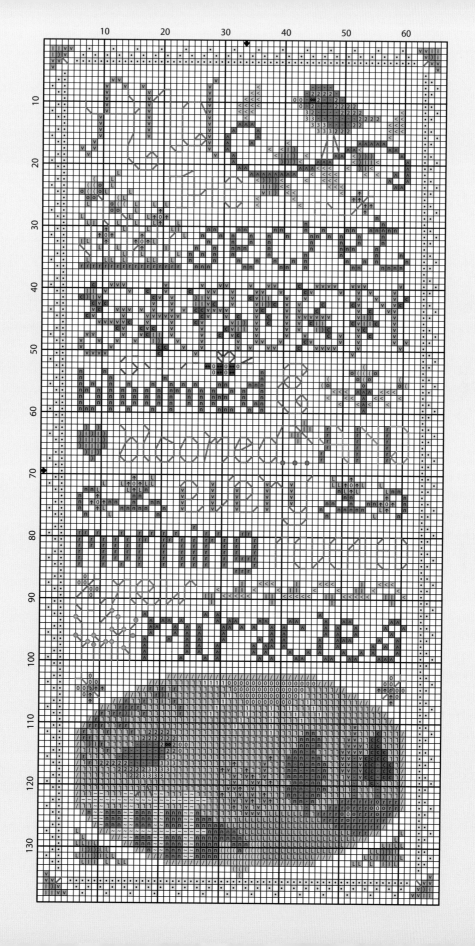

7

In Sunshine

I have to be honest: this happy design is probably one of my favorites in this book! I love sheep, so I always enjoy including them in my designs, and of course sunshine warms us, in both body and soul. Allow the gentle message of this design to warm you like the rays of the sun as you stitch this piece.

Fabric: 28-count Ivory Jobelan by Wichelt (stitched over 2 threads)
Stitch count: 85 wide x 85 high
Stitched size: 6 in. (15.4 cm) diameter

Cut fabric to measure at least 10 inches (25.4 cm) all around, and then fold in half and count out to start stitching at a suitable point. When stitching is done, wash and lightly iron it (if necessary), and then carefully trim the piece to measure at least 8½ inches (21.6 cm) in diameter. Insert the stitched piece into a wooden hoop measuring 7½ inches (19.1 cm) in diameter; make sure the fabric is lying flat and straight before tightening the hoop. Cover the back of the hoop with a circle of soft felt glued into place. (This step is optional, but it does hide the back of the stitching.) Use satin ribbon in a color of your choice to create a hanging loop for the hoop.

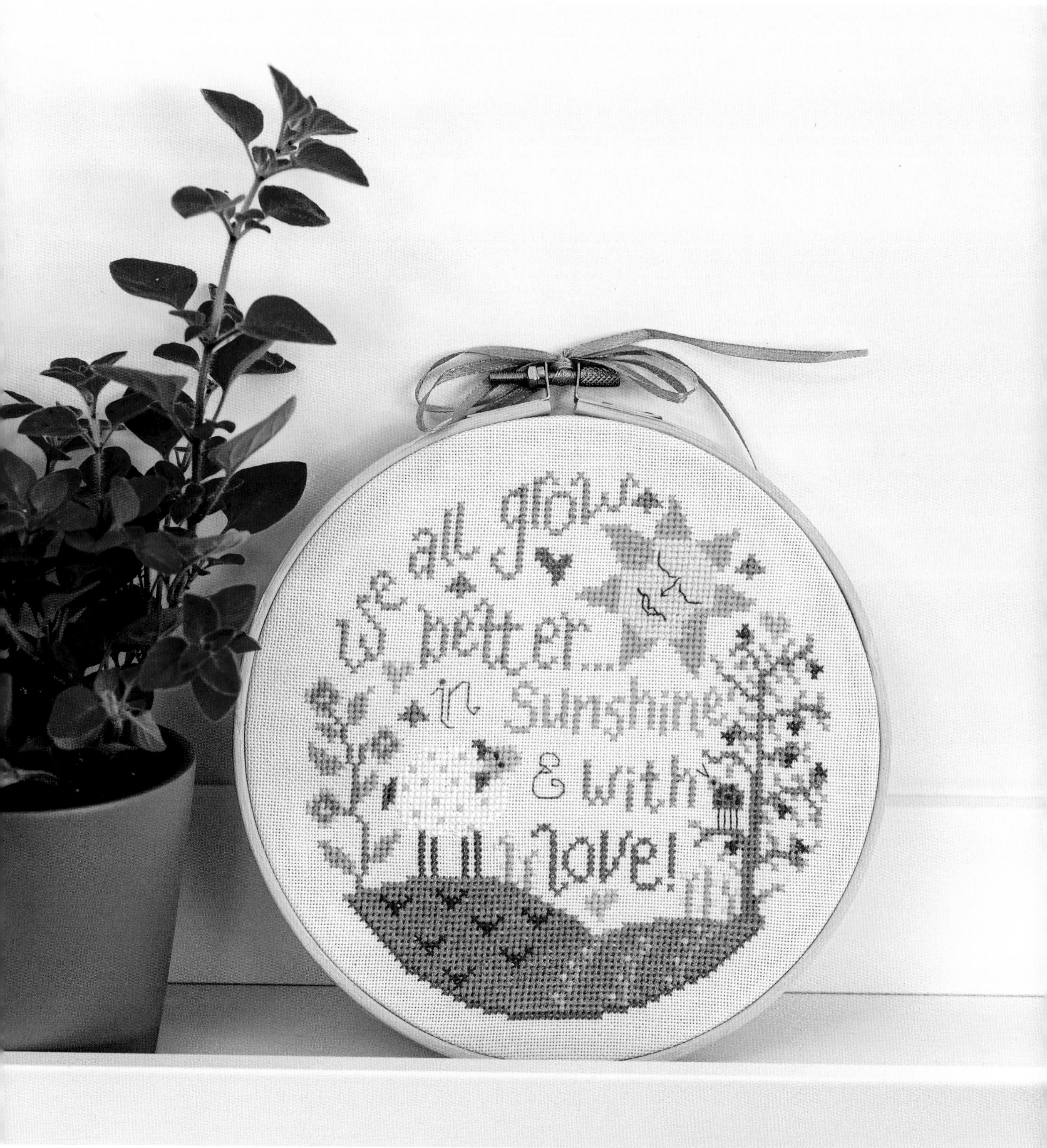

we all grow better... in Sunshine & with love!

Floss Used for Full Stitches:

Symbol		Strands	Type	Number	Color
	I	2	DMC	522	Fern Green
	~	2	DMC	524	Fern Green-VY LT
	(	2	DMC	640	Beige Gray-VY DK
	>	2	DMC	644	Beige Gray-MD
	c	2	DMC	760	Salmon
	0	2	DMC	761	Salmon-LT
	/	2	DMC	932	Antique Blue-LT
	3	2	DMC	3013	Khaki Green-LT
	⌐	2	DMC	3032	Mocha Brown-MD
	^	2	DMC	3362	Pine Green-DK
	o	2	DMC	3363	Pine Green-MD
	<	2	DMC	3364	Pine Green
	m	2	DMC	3712	Salmon-MD
	4	2	DMC	3771	Terra Cotta-UL VY LT
	-	2	DMC	3835	Grape-MD
	v	2	DMC	3836	Grape-LT
	n	2	DMC	3854	Autumn Gold-MD
	L	2	DMC	3855	Autumn Gold-LT
	)	2	DMC	3856	Mahogany-UL VY LT
	·	2	DMC	3865	Winter White

Floss Used for French Knots:

Symbol		Strands	Type	Number	Color
	●	1	DMC	931	Antique Blue-MD
	●	1	DMC	3787	Brown Gray-DK

Floss Used for Back Stitches:

Symbol		Strands	Type	Number	Color
	——	1	DMC	931	Antique Blue-MD
	——	1	DMC	3787	Brown Gray-DK

Herbs of Grace

This design was almost inevitable, given that I am also an herbalist and use herbs daily in my home, for both body and soul! No garden is complete without at least a few herbs, in my humble opinion—and even if you have only a windowsill, you can still cultivate a delightful herb garden at home! This design honors the old-fashioned and traditional herb garden, with its rows of gently fragrant plants, and would make a beautiful gift for any gardeners you know—or for yourself!

Even if you have never grown herbs before, the good news is that they are, in general, easy to grow, outdoors or indoors—provided they get plenty of light and moisture when needed. I have often been asked what my favorite herbs are and what I would recommend for beginning herb gardeners. My answer is that I have so many different favorite herbs that it's hard to make a choice, but I would have to say the following make a good initial foray into the herbal world: mint, thyme, chives, parsley, basil, and lavender—all have both medicinal and culinary uses. On a personal level, I would have to say that cilantro (coriander in the United Kingdom and elsewhere) is an essential herb for me, as I love cooking Eastern/Mexican food, for which this herb is a prerequisite. However, I do know some people really dislike the taste, so it's definitely an individual preference!

Herbal Salt Recipe

Herbal salts are a delicious way to use fresh herbs (and reduce your salt intake, which is generally a good thing, health-wise). These salts can be used in salad dressings, sauces, marinades, barbecue rubs, baking, and more. Herbs to choose include oregano, cilantro, rosemary, thyme, mint, or basil. Roughly chop up about 1 cup of your chosen fresh herb, and then place in a food processor or blender, together with 1 cup sea salt, grated zest of 1 small lemon, 1 peeled garlic clove, and 1 small chopped green chili (optional!). Blend the mixture well, and store in a covered glass jar in the refrigerator. The mixture will keep for a couple of weeks if stored correctly.

WESTEND61/WESTEND61 VIA GETTY IMAGES

Fabric: 28-count antique white Jobelan by Wichelt (stitched over 2 threads)
Stitch count: 97 wide x 71 high
Stitched size: 6¾ x 5 in. (17.2 x 12.7 cm)

Cut your fabric to measure at least 12 x 10 inches (30.5 x 25.4 cm); this will allow enough for finishing the design as a freestanding piece, as shown. Fold the fabric in half, and then count out to start stitching at a suitable point. When you have finished, wash and press the piece (if necessary) and trim any loose threads.

You will need two pieces of light foam core board (or similar), each measuring 5½ x 8 inches (14 x 20 cm). Glue a piece of soft white felt onto one of the pieces of board—doing so provides a little padding for the stitched piece. Cover the other piece of board with suitable light cotton patchwork fabric, and glue it around to the back. Center the stitched work on the felt-covered board and fold the excess fabric to the back tightly; make sure the design is centered and smooth, and then hold it in place on the back using double-sided tape. Glue the two panels together, right sides facing outward, and allow the glue to dry fully. Last of all, glue a length of satin ribbon right around the panel (to hide the join) and finish in a decorative bow on the top—I often use a couple of large, decorative pins to hold the bow in place.

Floss Used for Full Stitches:

Symbol		Strands	Type	Number	Color
	l	2	DMC	152	Shell Pink-MD LT
	m	2	DMC	223	Shell Pink-LT
	<	2	DMC	316	Antique Mauve-MD
	a	2	DMC	502	Blue Green
	c	2	DMC	522	Fern Green
	~	2	DMC	524	Fern Green-VY LT
	-	2	DMC	644	Beige Gray-MD
	v	2	DMC	676	Old Gold-LT
	·	2	DMC	822	Beige Gray-LT
	r	2	DMC	932	Antique Blue-LT
	(	2	DMC	3013	Khaki Green-LT
	L	2	DMC	3042	Antique Violet-LT
	)	2	DMC	3053	Green Gray
	n	2	DMC	3363	Pine Green-MD
	/	2	DMC	3364	Pine Green
	o	2	DMC	3727	Antique Mauve-LT
	>	2	DMC	3817	Celadon Green-LT

Floss Used for Half Stitches:

Symbol		Strands	Type	Number	Color
	>	2	DMC	3817	Celadon Green-LT

Floss Used for French Knots:

Symbol		Strands	Type	Number	Color
	●	1	DMC	640	Beige Gray-VY DK
	●	1	DMC	3727	Antique Mauve-LT

Floss Used for Back Stitches:

Symbol		Strands	Type	Number	Color
	——	1	DMC	502	Blue Green
	——	1	DMC	640	Beige Gray-VY DK
	——	1	DMC	3012	Khaki Green-MD
	——	1	DMC	3363	Pine Green-MD

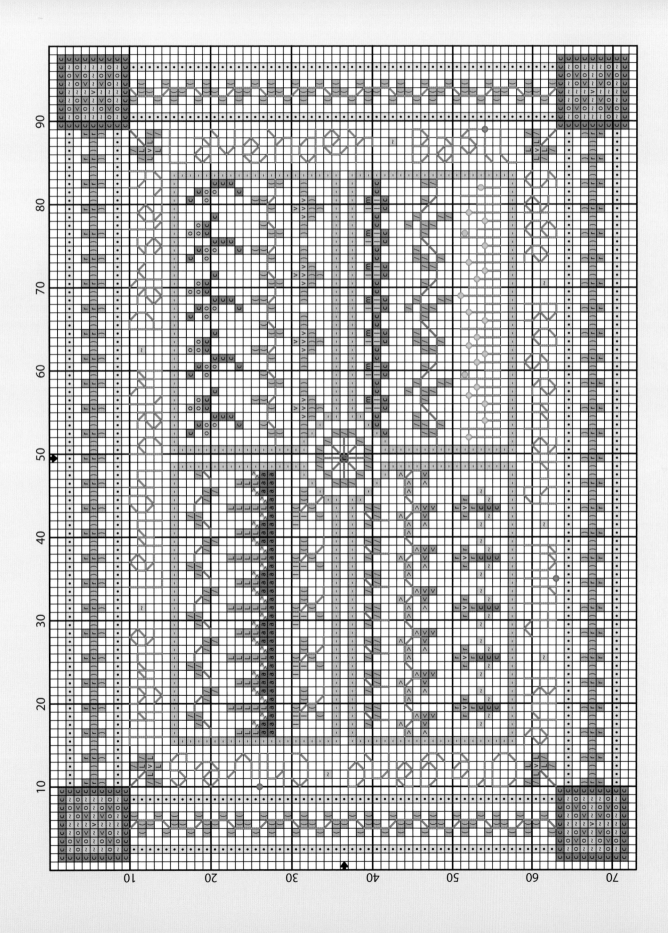

Flowers Are Happy Things

A simple and beautiful quote, and I have turned it into a pretty little stitchery. Finished as a mini pillow to grace your home, it could also be displayed in a basket or used to decorate a floral wreath or doorknob.

Fabric: 28-count antique white Jobelan (stitched over 2 threads)
Stitch count: 59 wide x 31 high
Stitched size: 4¼ x 2½ in. (10.8 x 6.4 cm)

Cut fabric at least 7 x 10 inches (17.8 x 25.4 cm), fold in half, and count out to start stitching at a suitable point. When done, wash and press lightly, and then carefully trim the piece so that you have at least ¾ inch (1.9 cm) of fabric extending all around the design. Cut two pieces of soft wool felt in a color of your choice, each measuring 4¼ x 7 inches (10.8 x 17.8 cm). Center the stitched piece on one of the felt pieces and stitch in place using a matching cotton thread and small running stitches. Place the two felt pieces together and stitch neatly all around the edges, using a small blanket stitch and 2 strands of embroidery floss in a coordinating color (be sure to leave an opening for filling). Lightly fill the little pillow with fiberfill, and then stitch the opening closed with blanket stitch. Add ribbons and buttons to the sides of the pillow, if desired.

Floss Used for Full Stitches:

Symbol		Strands	Type	Number	Color
	o	2	DMC	210	Lavender-MD
	+	2	DMC	211	Lavender-LT
	>	2	DMC	368	Pistachio Green-LT
	((	2	DMC	436	Tan
	<	2	DMC	522	Fern Green
	⌐	2	DMC	524	Fern Green-VY LT
	L	2	DMC	760	Salmon
	·	2	DMC	761	Salmon-LT
	c	2	DMC	931	Antique Blue-MD
	/	2	DMC	932	Antique Blue-LT
	~	2	DMC	3013	Khaki Green-LT
	∧	2	DMC	3364	Pine Green
	))	2	DMC	3854	Autumn Gold-MD
	I	2	DMC	3856	Mahogany-UL VY LT
	v	2	DMC	3862	Mocha Beige-DK

Floss Used for French Knots:

Symbol		Strands	Type	Number	Color
	●	1	DMC	436	Tan
	●	1	DMC	3712	Salmon-MD
	●	1	DMC	3856	Mahogany-UL VY LT

Floss Used for Back Stitches:

Symbol		Strands	Type	Number	Color
	——	1	DMC	436	Tan
	——	1	DMC	3012	Khaki Green-MD
	——	1	DMC	3363	Pine Green-MD
	——	1	DMC	3712	Salmon-MD
	——	1	DMC	3862	Mocha Beige-DK

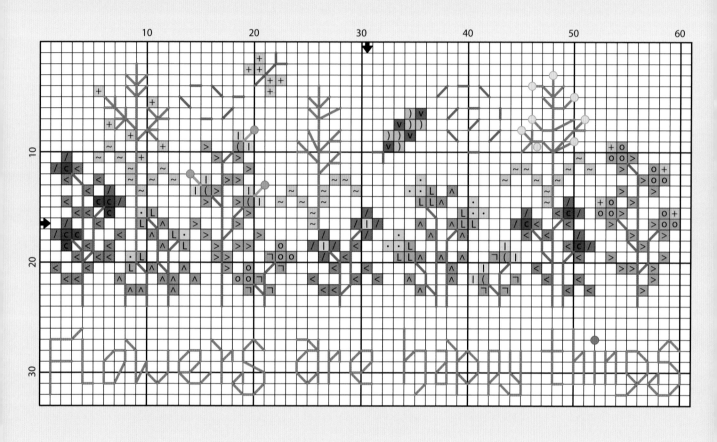

" Some people like to make a little garden out of life
and walk down a path . . ."

Jean Anouilh

Song of the Birds

This is one of my favorite quotes, and because I absolutely love birds and believe them to be one of earth's sweetest gifts to us, I really enjoyed creating this pretty design. (The quote has been attributed to several writers, but I chose to keep Maya Angelou's name on the design; she was such an inspiration to so many with her words and life.)

I am so fortunate to live in a cabin surrounded by trees, and birds are constant visitors to my deck (and their feeding tray!). It's become increasingly important in recent years to feed wild birds, since their living habitat has, in general, been badly impacted by humans' usage of the earth, building, and so on. If you don't already feed the birds, it's a good idea to familiarize yourself with some of the local species and what their diet should consist of; these days the general consensus is that birds should not be given bread, but rather seeds, nuts, and fruit. Particularly in winter, they need their food supplies to be supplemented, and it is also helpful to provide access to fresh water.

Fabric: 28-count Star Sapphire Jobelan by Wichelt (stitched over 2 threads)
Stitch count: 97 wide x 126 high
Stitched size: 7 x 9 in. (17.6 x 22.8 cm)

Cut fabric to measure at least 10 x 12 inches (25.4 cm), and then fold in half and count out to start stitching at a convenient point. (I would suggest doing the roof/house outline first; that gives a good frame of reference for the rest of the stitching.) When stitching is done, wash and press lightly (if necessary). This piece was finished as a simple hanging: Trim the design to around 1½ inches (3.8 cm) all around the stitched area, and then fold down the top and suspend the piece from a length of ribbon or cotton twine, using a few mini wooden clothespins to hold it in place.

Feed the Birds

My mom used to make little seed dishes for the birds: First, cut an orange in half and hollow out the centers. Melt lard and mix it with suitable bird seed and chopped nuts, and scoop the mixture into the centers of the orange halves. When the lard has hardened, make holes in three sides of the top of each orange piece with an awl, and thread loops of string or twine through. Use these to hang the oranges from suitable branches of trees or shrubs.

Floss Used for Full Stitches:

Symbol		Strands	Type	Number	Color
■	-	2	DMC	152	Shell Pink-MD LT
■	n	2	DMC	223	Shell Pink-LT
■	∧	2	DMC	316	Antique Mauve-MD
■	o	2	DMC	522	Fern Green
■	>	2	DMC	524	Fern Green-VY LT
■	<	2	DMC	676	Old Gold-LT
■	c	2	DMC	926	Gray Green-MD
■	/	2	DMC	927	Gray Green-LT
■	l	2	DMC	928	Gray Green-VY LT
■	v	2	DMC	3012	Khaki Green-MD
■	)	2	DMC	3013	Khaki Green-LT
■	e	2	DMC	3363	Pine Green-MD
■	r	2	DMC	3364	Pine Green
■	(	2	DMC	3727	Antique Mauve-LT
■	~	2	DMC	3773	Desert Sand-MD
■	#	2	DMC	3790	Beige Gray-UL DK
■	u	2	DMC	3828	Hazelnut Brown
■	s	2	DMC	3835	Grape-MD
■	L	2	DMC	3836	Grape-LT
■	∞	2	DMC	3854	Autumn Gold-MD
■	m	2	DMC	3863	Mocha Beige-MD
■	1	2	DMC	3864	Mocha Beige-LT
□	·	2	DMC	3865	Winter White

Floss Used for French Knots:

Symbol		Strands	Type	Number	Color
■	●	1	DMC	3768	Gray Green-DK
■	●	1	DMC	3828	Hazelnut Brown

Floss Used for Back Stitches:

Symbol		Strands	Type	Number	Color
■	———	1	DMC	522	Fern Green
■	———	1	DMC	3012	Khaki Green-MD
■	———	1	DMC	3363	Pine Green-MD
■	———	1	DMC	3768	Gray Green-DK
■	———	1	DMC	3790	Beige Gray-UL DK

Heart of a Rose

Soft colors of rose, antique mauve, and green create this sampler, an ode to what is arguably the most beautiful (and beloved) of all flowers. First cultivated at least 3,000 years ago in Iran, roses are known as the "queen of flowers" and offer a true multitude of uses, both practical and spiritual.

Roses are a symbol of love and friendship, as we all know, but, more than that, they can connect us with our deepest, most spiritual selves, clear the mind, and lift our spirits when we are feeling low or anxious. I strongly recommend always keeping a bottle of both rose water (rose hydrosol) and rose essential oil on hand; a few drops of the oil added to bathwater make for a truly beautiful experience! Rose water can be added to a mister and then sprayed to freshen and uplift the atmosphere in the bedroom or living room. In addition, dried rose petals (grown naturally without pesticides!) can be crumbled and included in herbal teas and other cool drinks. Culinary rose water (which is not the same as the rose hydrosol mentioned above) is widely used in the cooking of the Mediterranean and Middle East, and it adds a wonderful, gentle perfume to baked goods and desserts. (Just use it in moderation; otherwise it can be a little too much!)

"One may live without bread,
but not without roses."
Jean Richepin

Fabric: 28-count China Pearl Jobelan by Wichelt (stitched over 2 threads)
Stitch count: 95 wide x 98 high
Stitched size: 6¾ x 7 in. (17.2 x 17.8 cm)

Cut fabric to measure at least 10 inches (25.4 cm) all around, and then fold in half and count out to start stitching at a suitable point. When stitching is complete, wash and lightly press it (if necessary) and finish as desired. This design is presented as a flat piece, but it could be finished in a number of ways: framed, as a pillow, or as a mounted, freestanding piece.

Floss Used for Full Stitches:

Symbol		Strands	Type	Number	Color
	⌐	2	DMC	225	Shell Pink-UL VY LT
	n	2	DMC	316	Antique Mauve-MD
	<	2	DMC	368	Pistachio Green-LT
	L	2	DMC	522	Fern Green
	/	2	DMC	524	Fern Green-VY LT
	c	2	DMC	760	Salmon
	)	2	DMC	761	Salmon-LT
	·	2	DMC	822	Beige Gray-LT
	I	2	DMC	3013	Khaki Green-LT
	m	2	DMC	3032	Mocha Brown-MD
	o	2	DMC	3363	Pine Green-MD
	(	2	DMC	3364	Pine Green
	∧	2	DMC	3688	Mauve-MD
	-	2	DMC	3689	Mauve-LT
	~	2	DMC	3727	Antique Mauve-LT
	v	2	DMC	3782	Mocha Brown-LT
	r	2	DMC	3863	Mocha Beige-MD

Floss Used for Back Stitches:

Symbol		Strands	Type	Number	Color
	————	1	DMC	316	Antique Mauve-MD
	————	1	DMC	3013	Khaki Green-LT
	————	1	DMC	3363	Pine Green-MD
	————	1	DMC	3790	Beige Gray-UL DK

Ladybug Cottage

A piece of pure garden fantasy: I imagined a little ladybug taking up residence in this pretty teapot at the bottom of a colorful garden! Ladybugs are magical creatures and very beneficial in the garden, as well as apparently being much-loved pets of the fairies! So welcome them to your garden—and plant lots of marigolds and thyme, which ladybugs (and fairies) are very fond of.

Fabric: 28-count antique white Jobelan by Wichelt (stitched over 2 threads)
Stitch count: 89 wide x 71 high
Stitched size: 6½ x 5 in. (16.5 x 12.8 cm)

Cut fabric to measure at least 9 inches (22.9 cm) all around; fold in half and count out to start stitching at a convenient point. When stitching is done, wash and press lightly (if necessary). This design is presented as a flat piece, but it could be finished in a number of ways—as a framed piece, I think it would make a delightful addition to a child's room, or it could be turned into a charming pillow.

Floss Used for Full Stitches:

	Symbol	Strands	Type	Number	Color
	L	2	DMC	152	Shell Pink-MD LT
	+	2	DMC	223	Shell Pink-LT
	)	2	DMC	225	Shell Pink-UL VY LT
	T	2	DMC	316	Antique Mauve-MD
	e	2	DMC	415	Pearl Gray
	H	2	DMC	522	Fern Green
	(	2	DMC	524	Fern Green-VY LT
	n	2	DMC	642	Beige Gray-DK
	/	2	DMC	644	Beige Gray-MD
	v	2	DMC	729	Old Gold-MD
	0	2	DMC	754	Peach-LT
	·	2	DMC	822	Beige Gray-LT
	c	2	DMC	3012	Khaki Green-MD
	u	2	DMC	3041	Antique Violet-MD
	o	2	DMC	3042	Antique Violet-LT
	∧	2	DMC	3053	Green Gray
	l	2	DMC	3364	Pine Green
	r	2	DMC	3721	Shell Pink-DK
	>	2	DMC	3727	Antique Mauve-LT
	<	2	DMC	3774	Desert Sand-VL
	V	2	DMC	3799	Pewter Gray-VY DK
	m	2	DMC	3828	Hazelnut Brown
	~	2	DMC	3855	Autumn Gold-LT
	↑	2	DMC	3862	Mocha Beige-DK
	-	2	DMC	3863	Mocha Beige-MD
	˥	2	DMC	3864	Mocha Beige-LT
	1	2	DMC	3865	Winter White

Floss Used for Half Stitches:

	Symbol	Strands	Type	Number	Color
	#	2	DMC	414	Steel Gray-DK
	·	2	DMC	822	Beige Gray-LT

Floss Used for Quarter Stitches:

	Symbol	Strands	Type	Number	Color
	·	2	DMC	822	Beige Gray-LT

Floss Used for French Knots:

	Symbol	Strands	Type	Number	Color
	●	1	DMC	223	Shell Pink-LT
	●	1	DMC	3799	Pewter Gray-VY DK
	●	1	DMC	3862	Mocha Beige-DK

Floss Used for Back Stitches:

	Symbol	Strands	Type	Number	Color
	—	1	DMC	3363	Pine Green-MD
	—	1	DMC	3727	Antique Mauve-LT
	—	1	DMC	3799	Pewter Gray-VY DK
	—	1	DMC	3862	Mocha Beige-DK

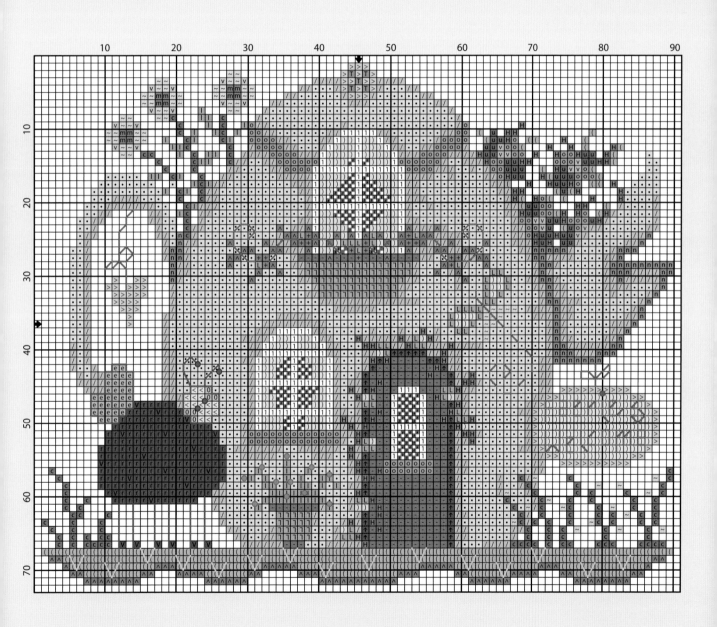

Love Is the Honey

I have always loved this quote by Victor Hugo and really enjoyed using it in this happy sampler, with its busy bees and little beehive! Bees are, of course, yet another of earth's gifts to us and need all our protection these days, given the erosion of their natural habitats, as well as unhealthy and unsustainable agricultural practices over the years, which have reduced their numbers dangerously.

Did you know that honey is the only foodstuff that does not spoil? Honey has been found in Egyptian tombs dating back several thousand years; it had become a little crystallized but was still edible. And it's just delicious in so many ways!

Fabric: 28-count Country French Linen in Mocha by Wichelt (stitched over 2 threads)
Stitch count: 125 wide x 65 high
Stitched size: 8¾ x 4½ in. (22.7 x 11.7 cm)

Cut the fabric to measure at least 12 x 8 inches (30.5 x 20.3 cm; this fabric has a greater tendency to fray); fold in half and count out to start stitching at a suitable point. When stitching is completed, wash (if necessary) and press lightly with a steam iron on the back of the stitching. This design is presented as a flat piece but can be finished in a number of different, creative ways: framed, as a pillow, or made into a freestanding, decorative piece (see the instructions for "Plant Your Garden" on page 57).

Herb-Infused Honey Recipe

If you can, always buy locally produced and organic (raw) honey. It may cost a little more, but not only are you helping the bees and farmers in your area, but the reality is that cheaper honey is often adulterated with sugar and other unwanted additives. And you can add to the natural goodness of honey by infusing it with herbs; such honeys can be used in the kitchen but also taken internally or used on the skin to counteract infections or irritation. Herbs to try include peppermint, sage, lavender, thyme, rose petals, lemon balm, rose geranium, and oregano.

Fill a large, sterilized glass jar with about 1½ cups chopped fresh herbs or about half that quantity of dried herb material. Pour over enough raw honey to completely cover the plant material. Cover and seal the jar, and leave it in a warm, dark place to infuse for 4–6 weeks. Then carefully strain out all the plant material and store the honey in a smaller glass jar. (If there is any mold on the honey, unfortunately you will need to discard it.) This honey should be stored in glass jars and kept in a cool, dark cupboard.

Floss Used for Full Stitches:

	Symbol	Strands	Type	Number	Color
	1	2	DMC	19	Bright Yellow
	-	2	DMC	352	Coral-LT
	c	2	DMC	356	Terra Cotta-MD
	v	2	DMC	407	Desert Sand-DK
	0	2	DMC	422	Hazelnut Brown-LT
	u	2	DMC	434	Brown-LT
	a	2	DMC	535	Ash Gray-VY LT
	<	2	DMC	676	Old Gold-LT
	∧	2	DMC	3012	Khaki Green-MD
	(	2	DMC	3013	Khaki Green-LT
	2	2	DMC	3032	Mocha Brown-MD
	L	2	DMC	3052	Green Gray-MD
	~	2	DMC	3072	Beaver Gray-VY LT
	¬	2	DMC	3348	Yellow Green-LT
	>	2	DMC	3364	Pine Green
	+	2	DMC	3771	Terra Cotta-UL VY LT
	l	2	DMC	3774	Desert Sand-VY LT
	n	2	DMC	3828	Hazelnut Brown
	e	2	DMC	3835	Grape-MD
	m	2	DMC	3836	Grape-LT
	)	2	DMC	3854	Autumn Gold-MD
	o	2	DMC	3862	Mocha Beige-DK
	·	2	DMC	3865	Winter White

Floss Used for Half Stitches:

	Symbol	Strands	Type	Number	Color
	0	2	DMC	422	Hazelnut Brown-LT
	a	2	DMC	535	Ash Gray-VY LT
	o	2	DMC	3862	Mocha Beige-DK

Floss Used for Quarter Stitches:

	Symbol	Strands	Type	Number	Color
	0	2	DMC	422	Hazelnut Brown-LT

Floss Used for French Knots:

	Symbol	Strands	Type	Number	Color
	●	1	DMC	535	Ash Gray-VY LT

Floss Used for Back Stitches:

	Symbol	Strands	Type	Number	Color
	——	1	DMC	535	Ash Gray-VY LT
	——	1	DMC	3052	Green Gray-MD
	——	1	DMC	3862	Mocha Beige-DK

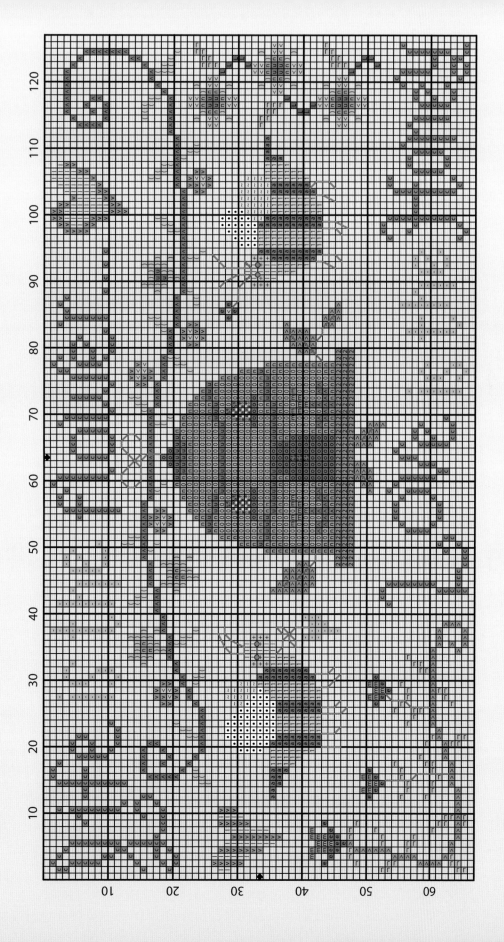

43

Cathy's Garden Quilt

As I said in the introduction, my mom's garden was a truly magical place when I was growing up, and my favorite place to spend time! But she was also a very gifted stitcher, who not only did embroidery but also made simple quilts, often embellished with little stitches and sayings. This design was created as a tribute to my mother, with thanks for the many lessons she taught me—about everything! I also like the fact that this design is versatile, and the individual elements can be used in various creative ways—imagine a collection of little pillows or scented sachets, each featuring one of these blocks.

Fabric: 28-count Waterlily Jobelan by Wichelt (stitched over 2 threads)
Stitch count: 93 wide x 93 high
Stitched size: 6½ x 6½ in. (16.8 x 16.8 cm)

Cut fabric at least 10 inches (25.4 cm) square, and then fold in half and count out to start your stitching at a suitable point—for this design, it's easier to stitch the border first, and then do the squares. When stitching is done, wash and press the work lightly (if necessary); then trim the piece so that you have 2 inches (5.1 cm) extra at the sides and bottom and 3½ inches (8.9 cm) at the top (to allow for the top fold-over). Stitch a neat hem all the way around the piece (½ inch/1.27 cm seam), using a suitable coordinating cotton thread. Fold the top down ¾ inch (1.9 cm), and hold in place with a few stitches on each side. Thread a suitable ribbon through the fold and hold the little "quilt" in place with a few tiny clothespins.

Floss Used for Full Stitches:

Symbol		Strands	Type	Number	Color
	I	2	DMC	152	Shell Pink-MD LT
	c	2	DMC	223	Shell Pink-LT
	n	2	DMC	316	Antique Mauve-MD
	o	2	DMC	522	Fern Green
	L	2	DMC	524	Fern Green-VY LT
	-	2	DMC	644	Beige Gray-MD
	~	2	DMC	676	Old Gold-LT
	>	2	DMC	778	Antique Mauve-VY LT
	^	2	DMC	3041	Antique Violet-MD
	/	2	DMC	3042	Antique Violet-LT
	v	2	DMC	3053	Green Gray
	)	2	DMC	3363	Pine Green-MD
	(	2	DMC	3364	Pine Green
	<	2	DMC	3727	Antique Mauve-LT
	·	2	DMC	3865	Winter White

Floss Used for Back Stitches:

Symbol		Strands	Type	Number	Color
		1	DMC	522	Fern Green
		1	DMC	640	Beige Gray-VY DK
		1	DMC	3363	Pine Green-MD

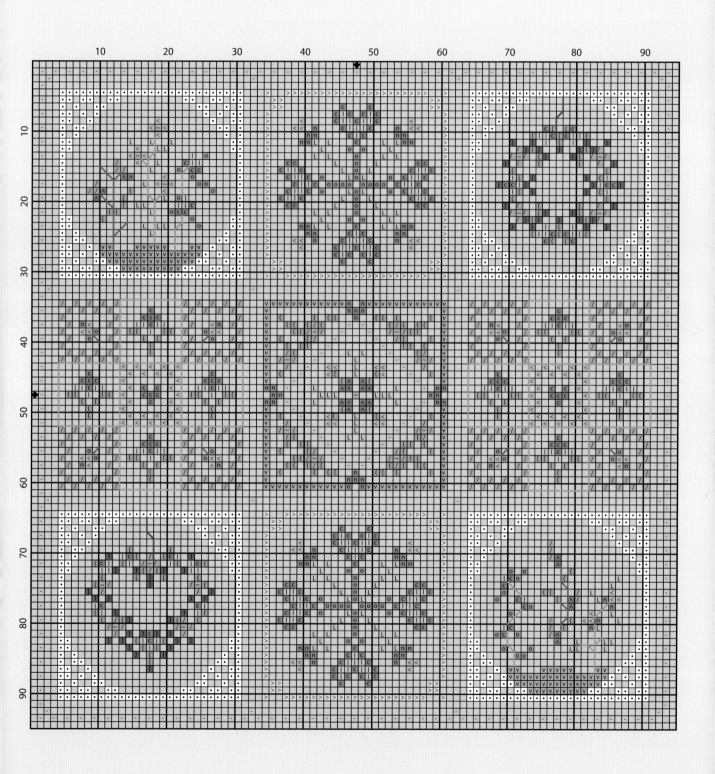

Earth Is a Garden

Another quote from *The Secret Garden*—and, of course, this is so true. We are surrounded by green magic everywhere (even in the most unlikely of places)—have you ever seen a wildflower poking up through a city sidewalk? I think the most important thing we can do is to always be aware, to notice the simple beauty happening all around us. This little stitched piece is a gentle reminder of that idea.

Fabric: 28-count China Pearl Jobelan by Wichelt (stitched over 2 threads)
Stitch count: 53 wide x 53 high
Stitched size: 3¾ x 3¾ in. (9.6 x 9.6 cm)

Cut fabric at least 7 inches (17.8 cm) square; fold in half and count out to start stitching at a convenient point. When stitching is complete, wash and press lightly (if necessary), and then carefully trim the fabric to measure 5¾ inches (14.6 cm) all around, ensuring that the stitched area is central. Cut a piece of suitable coordinating cotton patchwork fabric to measure the same size, and then pin both pieces together (right sides facing inward). Starting at one side, stitch the pieces together with a small running stitch (allowing a ½-inch/1.27-cm seam), leaving an opening at one side for filling the pillow. Turn the stitching right side out and stuff lightly with fiberfill, and then neatly stitch the opening closed. Add ribbons on either side (and buttons/charms) if desired.

Floss Used for Full Stitches:

Symbol		Strands	Type	Number	Color
☐	L	2	DMC	353	Peach
☐	∧	2	DMC	676	Old Gold-LT
☐	·	2	DMC	822	Beige Gray-LT
☐	↑	2	DMC	3013	Khaki Green-LT
☐	(	2	DMC	3041	Antique Violet-MD
☐	)	2	DMC	3042	Antique Violet-LT
☐	v	2	DMC	3053	Green Gray
☐	n	2	DMC	3363	Pine Green-MD
☐	-	2	DMC	3364	Pine Green
☐	/	2	DMC	3774	Desert Sand-V LT
☐	o	2	DMC	3778	Terra Cotta-LT
☐	c	2	DMC	3863	Mocha Beige-MD

Floss Used for French Knots:

Symbol		Strands	Type	Number	Color
☐	●	1	DMC	3041	Antique Violet-MD

Floss Used for Back Stitches:

Symbol		Strands	Type	Number	Color
☐	▬▬▬	1	DMC	3011	Khaki Green-DK
☐	———	1	DMC	3041	Antique Violet-MD
☐	———	1	DMC	3363	Pine Green-MD

Sweet Petals

Not far from my home there is a farmers' market held several times a month, and it is one of my favorite places to visit! I especially love the little flower stall, with its potted herbs and bunches of bright flowers. It's both visually and spiritually heartwarming to spend a few moments there, and I created this simple but colorful design as a tribute to the flower stall and the delightful woman, Jo, who owns it.

Even if you don't have your own garden to cultivate, I urge you to seek out farmers' markets or flower farms—there is certain to be one within reach—and visit them. It's a beautiful outing all by itself, and I can guarantee you will come home with an armful of fresh blooms to beautify your home and make you smile!

Fabric: 28-count antique white Jobelan by Wichelt (stitched over 2 threads)
Stitch count: 69 wide x 68 high
Stitched size: 5 inches (12.7 cm) in diameter

Cut fabric to measure at least 10 inches square (25.4 cm); fold in half and count out to start stitching at a convenient point. When stitching is finished, wash it (if necessary) and press lightly with a steam iron. This design was finished in a wooden hoop measuring 6½ inches (16.5 cm) in diameter; trim the stitched piece in a circle at least 1½ inches (3.8 cm) larger than the hoop, and insert it, making sure the piece is centered and flat before you tighten the hoop. You can cover the back of the hoop with a piece of thin felt, glued in place, to hide the back of the stitching. Finish the hoop with a ribbon for hanging.

Floss Used for Full Stitches:

Symbol		Strands	Type	Number	Color
	r	2	DMC	317	Pewter Gray
	)	2	DMC	414	Steel Gray-DK
	m	2	DMC	435	Brown-VY LT
	1	2	DMC	437	Tan-LT
	o	2	DMC	522	Fern Green
	<	2	DMC	524	Fern Green-VY LT
	a	2	DMC	744	Yellow-Pale
	c	2	DMC	760	Salmon
	-	2	DMC	761	Salmon-LT
	n	2	DMC	926	Gray Green-MD
	/	2	DMC	927	Gray Green-LT
	u	2	DMC	3012	Khaki Green-MD
	T	2	DMC	3013	Khaki Green-LT
	v	2	DMC	3363	Pine Green-MD
	^	2	DMC	3364	Pine Green
	L	2	DMC	3688	Mauve-MD
	~	2	DMC	3689	Mauve-LT
	>	2	DMC	3835	Grape-MD
	((	2	DMC	3836	Grape-LT
	I	2	DMC	3863	Mocha Beige-MD
	⌐	2	DMC	3864	Mocha Beige-LT
	·	2	DMC	3865	Winter White

Floss Used for French Knots:

Symbol		Strands	Type	Number	Color
	●	1	DMC	317	Pewter Gray
	●	1	DMC	761	Salmon-LT
	●	1	DMC	3688	Mauve-MD
	●	1	DMC	3835	Grape-MD

Floss Used for Back Stitches:

Symbol		Strands	Type	Number	Color
	▬	1	DMC	317	Pewter Gray
	▬	1	DMC	414	Steel Gray-DK
	▬	1	DMC	3363	Pine Green-MD
	▬	1	DMC	3835	Grape-MD

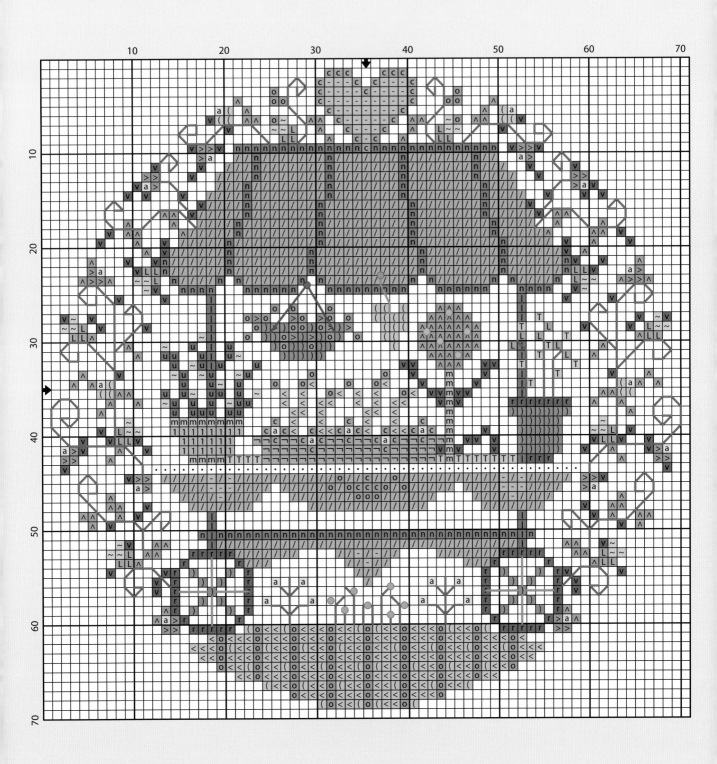

Plant Your Garden

This piece features another favorite saying of mine (credited to Luther Burbank). This is quite a colorful piece that serves as a reminder of the power we all possess to make our gardens—and our lives—beautiful and unique!

Fabric: 28-count Café Mocha Country French Linen by Wichelt (stitched over 2 threads)
Stitch count: 101 wide x 58 high
Stitched size: 7¼ x 4¼ in (18.3 x 10.7 cm)

Cut fabric to measure at least 11 x 7 inches (27.9 x 17.8 cm), and then fold in half and count out to start stitching at a convenient point. When stitching is complete, wash and press lightly (if necessary) and trim any loose threads. Cut a piece of light foam core board measuring 8½ x 5½ inches (21.6 x 14 cm) and glue a piece of soft white felt (or similar fabric) to the top of the board. Stretch the stitched piece over the covered board, ensuring that it is centered and straight, and then fold the excess fabric neatly to the back of the board and hold in place with double-sided tape. Cut a piece of felt or other suitable fabric, and glue it to the back of the board to hide the fabric/tape. Add a loop of ribbon and a button to the top as a finishing touch!

Floss Used for Full Stitches:

Symbol		Strands	Type	Number	Color
	I	2	DMC	152	Shell Pink-MD LT
	v	2	DMC	223	Shell Pink-LT
	∧	2	DMC	316	Antique Mauve-MD
	n	2	DMC	502	Blue Green
	>	2	DMC	522	Fern Green
	r	2	DMC	676	Old Gold-LT
	••	2	DMC	930	Antique Blue-DK
	c	2	DMC	931	Antique Blue-MD
	-	2	DMC	932	Antique Blue-LT
	o	2	DMC	3053	Green Gray
	••	2	DMC	3363	Pine Green-MD
	~	2	DMC	3364	Pine Green
	(	2	DMC	3727	Antique Mauve-LT
	/	2	DMC	3817	Celadon Green-LT
	)	2	DMC	3835	Grape-MD
	<	2	DMC	3836	Grape-LT
	u	2	DMC	3863	Mocha Beige-MD
	·	2	DMC	3864	Mocha Beige-LT

Floss Used for French Knots:

Symbol		Strands	Type	Number	Color
	●	1	DMC	676	Old Gold-LT
	●	1	DMC	930	Antique Blue-DK

Floss Used for Back Stitches:

Symbol		Strands	Type	Number	Color
	——	1	DMC	930	Antique Blue-DK
	——	1	DMC	3363	Pine Green-MD
	——	1	DMC	3863	Mocha Beige-MD

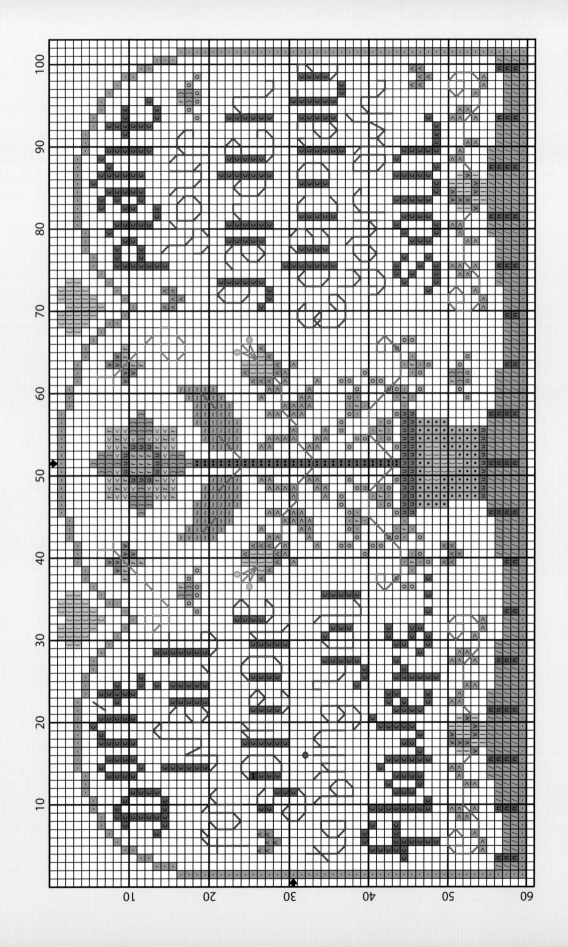

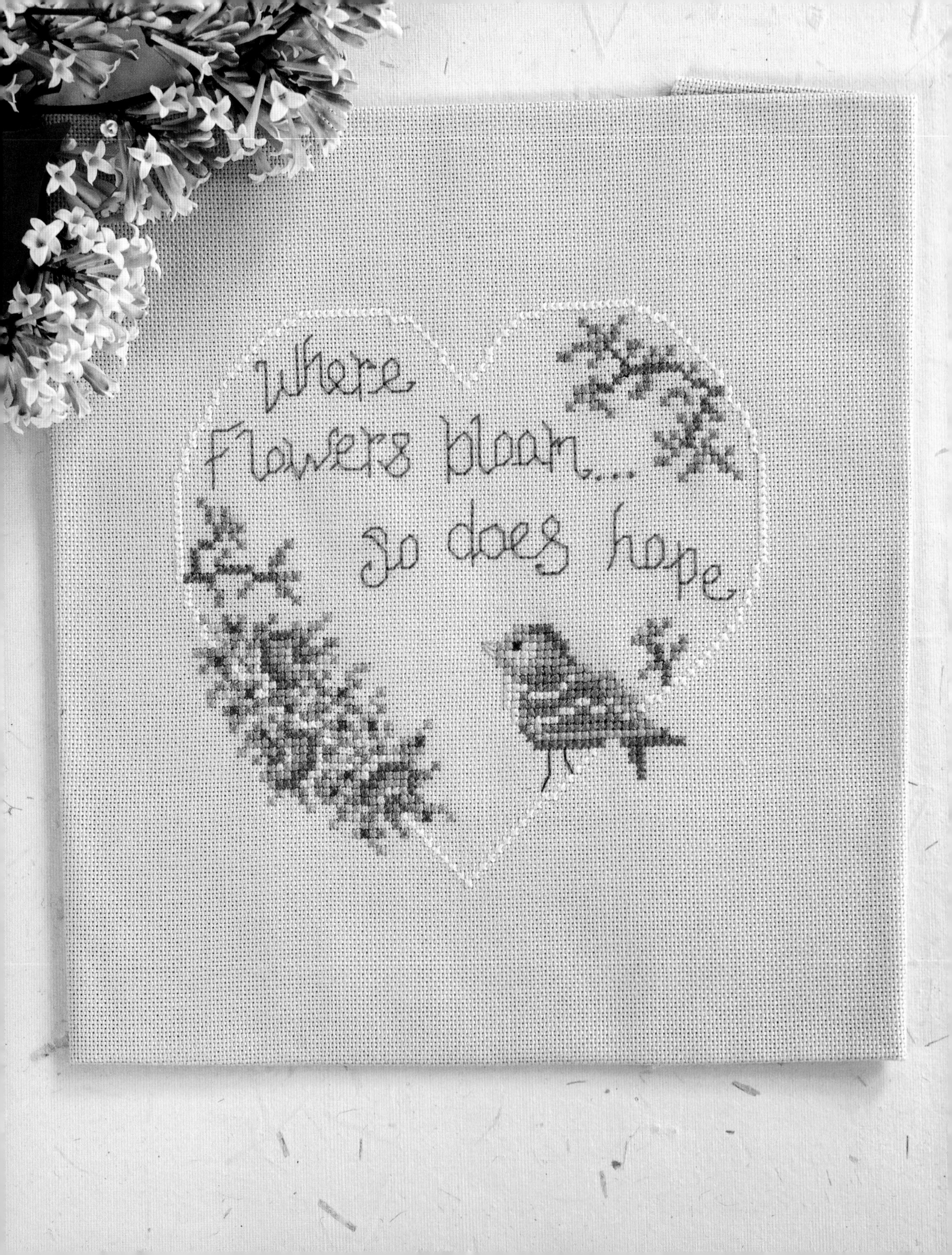
Where
Flowers bloom...
so does hope

Where Flowers Bloom . . .

The simplicity and quiet beauty of this piece make it very special to me, as does the little bird! It's a design that would make a beautiful addition to any home or a very special gift for someone who has been experiencing difficulties in their life and needs to be reminded of just how important and powerful hope can be!

Fabric: 28-count Star Sapphire Jobelan by Wichelt (stitched over 2 threads)
Stitch count: 75 wide x 69 high
Stitched size: 5½ x 5 in. (13.6 x 12.5 cm)

Cut fabric to measure at least 9 inches (22.9 cm) square, and then fold in half and count out to start stitching at a convenient place. When stitching is complete, wash and press lightly (if necessary) and finish the piece as desired. Here the design is shown as a flat piece, but it would be delightful either framed or stitched up as a pillow; it could also be turned into a stitched book/journal cover.

Floss Used for Full Stitches:

Symbol		Strands	Type	Number	Color
	-	2	DMC	152	Shell Pink-MD LT
	■	2	DMC	223	Shell Pink-LT
	l	2	DMC	225	Shell Pink-UL VY LT
	o	2	DMC	522	Fern Green
	>	2	DMC	524	Fern Green-VY LT
	⊗	2	DMC	640	Beige Gray-VY DK
	1	2	DMC	642	Beige Gray-DK
	/	2	DMC	676	Old Gold-LT
	<	2	DMC	3042	Antique Violet-LT
	n	2	DMC	3052	Green Gray-MD
	v	2	DMC	3726	Antique Mauve-DK
	L	2	DMC	3727	Antique Mauve-LT
	∧	2	DMC	3774	Desert Sand V LT
	r	2	DMC	3856	Mahogany-UL VY LT
	(	2	DMC	3863	Mocha Beige-MD
	)	2	DMC	3864	Mocha Beige-LT
	·	2	DMC	3865	Winter White
	2	2	DMC	3866	Mocha Brown-UL VY LT

Floss Used for French Knots:

Symbol		Strands	Type	Number	Color
	●	1	DMC	640	Beige Gray-VY DK

Floss Used for Back Stitches:

Symbol		Strands	Type	Number	Color
	——	1	DMC	640	Beige Gray-VY DK
	——	1	DMC	3853	Autumn Gold-DK

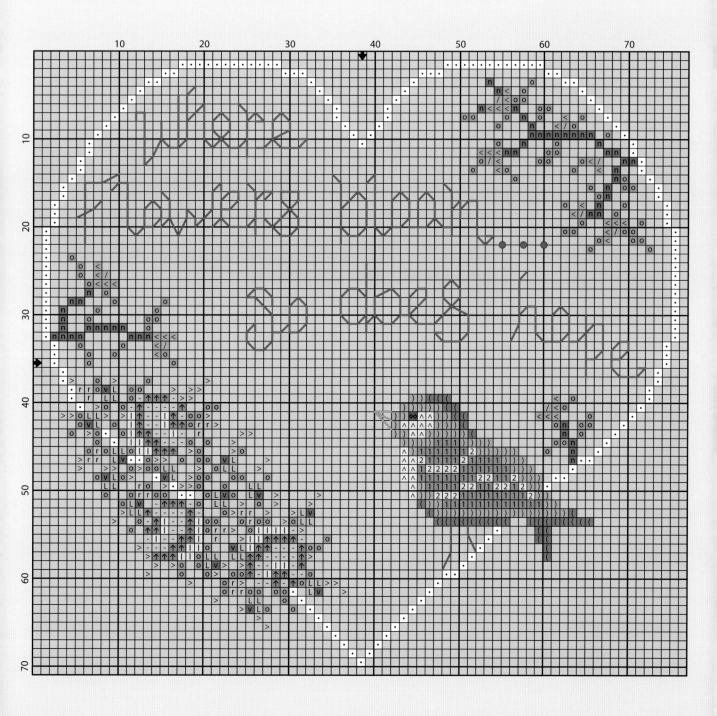

Tea in My Garden

Is anything nicer than a sunny afternoon spent in a pretty, scented garden with loved ones and friends, sipping tea and eating cake as the hours go peacefully by? I, for one, can't imagine a lovelier way to spend my time, and I created this colorful sampler as a reminder of these happy hours.

Fabric: 28-count Bone Jobelan by Wichelt (stitched over 2 threads)
Stitch count: 58 wide x 106 high
Stitched size: 4¼ x 7¼ in. (10.8 x 18.4 cm)

Cut fabric to measure at least 7 inches wide x 12 inches high (17.8 x 30.5 cm). Fold in half and count out to start stitching at a suitable point—I would suggest stitching the border first. When stitching is complete, wash and press lightly (if necessary). This design is presented as a flat piece, but I would suggest that it would look great framed or finished as a wall hanging (as in "The Secret Garden" design on page 2).

Herbal Tea

One of the simplest and most delicious ways to enjoy the benefits of plants and herbs is to brew them into teas (also known as tisanes). Obviously, it's possible to buy many different herbal tea blends these days, but it's very rewarding to create your own or to add some of your own herbs to regular teas. (Just make sure the herbs you choose are organically grown without pesticides and safe for consumption.) Some good herbs for teas include mint, lavender, jasmine, chamomile (particularly good for stress and insomnia), rosemary, and sage. Rooibos tea, which is native to my home country of South Africa, is a powerful antioxidant and anti-aging herb!

Floss Used for Full Stitches:

Symbol		Strands	Type	Number	Color
	I	2	DMC	30	Violet-Blue
	~	2	DMC	210	Lavender-MD
	(	2	DMC	320	Pistachio Green-MD
	^	2	DMC	341	Blue Violet-LT
	⌐	2	DMC	368	Pistachio Green-LT
	<	2	DMC	436	Tan
	L	2	DMC	502	Blue Green
	/	2	DMC	503	Blue Green-MD
	c	2	DMC	553	Violet
	n	2	DMC	644	Beige Gray-MD
	>	2	DMC	744	Yellow-Pale
	o	2	DMC	760	Salmon
	-	2	DMC	761	Salmon-LT
	+	2	DMC	822	Beige Gray-LT
	v	2	DMC	3712	Salmon-MD
	·	2	DMC	3865	Winter White

Floss Used for Back Stitches:

Symbol		Strands	Type	Number	Color
	———	1	DMC	520	Fern Green-DK
	———	1	DMC	640	Beige Gray-VY DK

69

A Butterfly Blessing

Butterflies are some of the most beautiful visitors we can have in our gardens. Full of color and grace, they are truly a marvel of nature. More than that, they are a powerful symbol of beauty, hope, and eternity; for this reason, they have been honored and loved by many different cultures and belief systems over the centuries. I am blessed enough to live in a place that is literally teeming with butterflies in the summer, so this little design was really quite inevitable!

Fabric: 28-count China Pearl Jobelan by Wichelt (stitched over 2 threads)
Stitch count: 67 wide x 67 high
Stitched size: 5 x 5 in. (12.7 x 12.7 cm)

Cut the fabric to measure at least 10 inches (25.4 cm) all around, and then fold in half and count out from the center to start stitching. (For designs like this one, it's generally easier to stitch the borders first.) When stitching is completed, add the beads as indicated on the chart, and then wash and press lightly (if necessary). Trim the fabric so that you have an additional 1½ inches (3.8 cm) around the stitched piece—thus you should have a piece measuring approximately 8 inches (20.3 cm) square.

Cut a piece of cotton patchwork fabric in similar colors (or plain) to the same size, and pin the two pieces together, right sides facing. Stitch them together with a running stitch, leaving an opening for turning. Turn to the right side and stuff lightly with fiberfill before sewing the opening closed. Cut two matching lengths of satin ribbon of your choice and stitch one to each side of the top of the pillow. I had two lovely antique butterfly charms that I added to each ribbon, but you can add buttons, too.

Butterfly Garden

Pollinators (which include butterflies, bees, moths, beetles, bats, and hummingbirds) are vitally important to our ecosystems and life on this planet in general, but much of their habitat is under threat or has been destroyed by chemicals and climate change. We can make our gardens, small or large, a haven for these precious little garden allies by choosing plants that will attract and sustain them. These include asters, bee balm, borage, cosmos, echinacea (coneflower), lavender, alyssum, salvia, and yarrow—also any flowers, like honeysuckle, that produce nectar.

DEBRALEE WISEBERG/E+ VIA GETTY IMAGES

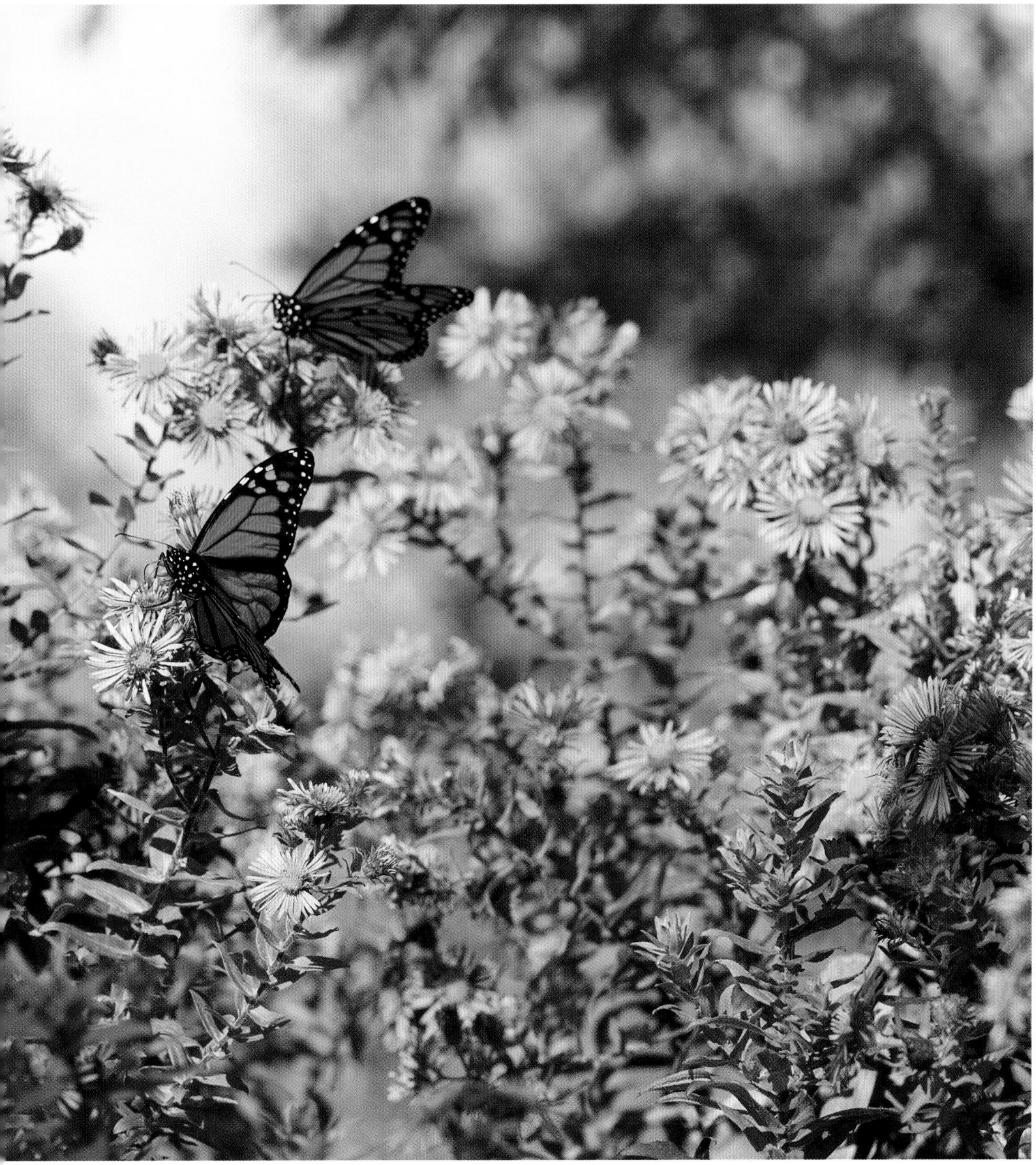

Floss Used for Full Stitches:

Symbol		Strands	Type	Number	Color
☐	))	2	DMC	24	Very Pale Mauve
☐	-	2	DMC	225	Shell Pink-UL VY LT
▣	o	2	DMC	316	Antique Mauve-MD
▣	c	2	DMC	642	Beige Gray-DK
▢	I	2	DMC	644	Beige Gray-MD
☐	L	2	DMC	778	Antique Mauve-VY LT
▢	+	2	DMC	3042	Antique Violet-LT
☐	~	2	DMC	3774	Desert Sand-VY LT
☐	·	2	DMC	3865	Winter White
▢	/	2	DMC	26	Pale Mauve

Floss Used for Quarter Stitches:

Symbol		Strands	Type	Number	Color
☐	~	2	DMC	3774	Desert Sand-VY LT

Floss Used for French Knots:

Symbol		Strands	Type	Number	Color
■	●	1	DMC	640	Beige Gray-VY DK

Floss Used for Back Stitches:

Symbol		Strands	Type	Number	Color
■	▬▬▬	1	DMC	640	Beige Gray-VY DK
▣	▬▬▬	1	DMC	3041	Antique Violet-MD
▢	▬▬▬	1	DMC	3778	Terra Cotta-LT

Beads Used:

Symbol		Type	Number	Color
☐	○	MH PGS Bead	40479	White

How to Be a Sunflower

A few years ago, we were traveling on a long-distance bus, and in the early morning we came over a hill to the incredibly beautiful sight of fields of sunflowers, stretching as far as the eye could see, turning their golden faces to the rising sun. Everyone on the bus fell silent. It was a truly magical moment—one I have always held in my heart. I decided to include a happy chicken in this design because not only do I love them, but they also seem to be such a bright symbol of hope and promise in the new day!

Sunflowers (their botanical name comes from the Greek god of the sun, Helios) are instantly recognizable the world over, and they also offer many gifts on both a practical and a spiritual level. This bright flower is linked to happiness, joy, and increased energy levels. We need the sun to stay healthy in body and mind, and sunflowers can also help improve our overall well-being. Growing just a few sunflowers in your garden brings added vitality and vibrance to your surroundings. (And please don't forget to use the sunflower seeds when your plants have reached the time of harvest. They are great for cooking or baking or just eating out of hand—and the birds love them too!)

Fabric: 28-count Ivory Jobelan by Wichelt (stitched over 2 threads)
Stitch count: 63 wide x 108 high
Stitched size: 4½ x 7¾ in. (11.4 x 19.6 cm)

Cut fabric to measure at least 7 by 11 inches (17.8 x 27.9 cm), and then fold in half and count out to start stitching at a suitable point—I recommend doing the border first; that makes placement of the other design elements easier. When stitching is complete, wash and lightly press the work (if necessary). This design is presented as a flat piece and can be finished as desired—framed or turned into a small hanging trimmed with yellow and green ribbons.

Floss Used for Full Stitches:

Symbol	Symbol	Strands	Type	Number	Color
	⌐	2	DMC	153	Violet-VY LT
	>	2	DMC	356	Terra Cotta-MD
	o	2	DMC	436	Tan
	0	2	DMC	437	Tan-LT
	^	2	DMC	729	Old Gold-MD
	1	2	DMC	738	Tan-VY LT
	)	2	DMC	3012	Khaki Green-MD
	c	2	DMC	3347	Yellow Green-MD
	~	2	DMC	3348	Yellow Green-LT
	L	2	DMC	3362	Pine Green-DK
	I	2	DMC	3771	Terra Cotta-UL VY LT
	n	2	DMC	3778	Terra Cotta-LT
	a	2	DMC	3836	Grape-LT
	<	2	DMC	3854	Autumn Gold-MD
	r	2	DMC	3855	Autumn Gold-LT
	/	2	DMC	3856	Mahogany-UL VY LT
	-	2	DMC	3862	Mocha Beige-DK
	·	2	DMC	3865	Winter White

Floss Used for French Knots:

Symbol	Symbol	Strands	Type	Number	Color
	●	1	DMC	535	Ash Gray-VY LT

Floss Used for Back Stitches:

Symbol	Symbol	Strands	Type	Number	Color
	▬▬▬	1	DMC	356	Terra Cotta-MD
	▬▬▬	1	DMC	535	Ash Gray-VY LT
	▬▬▬	1	DMC	3011	Khaki Green-DK
	▬▬▬	1	DMC	3362	Pine Green-DK
	▬▬▬	1	DMC	3835	Grape-MD
	▬▬▬	1	DMC	3854	Autumn Gold-MD

81

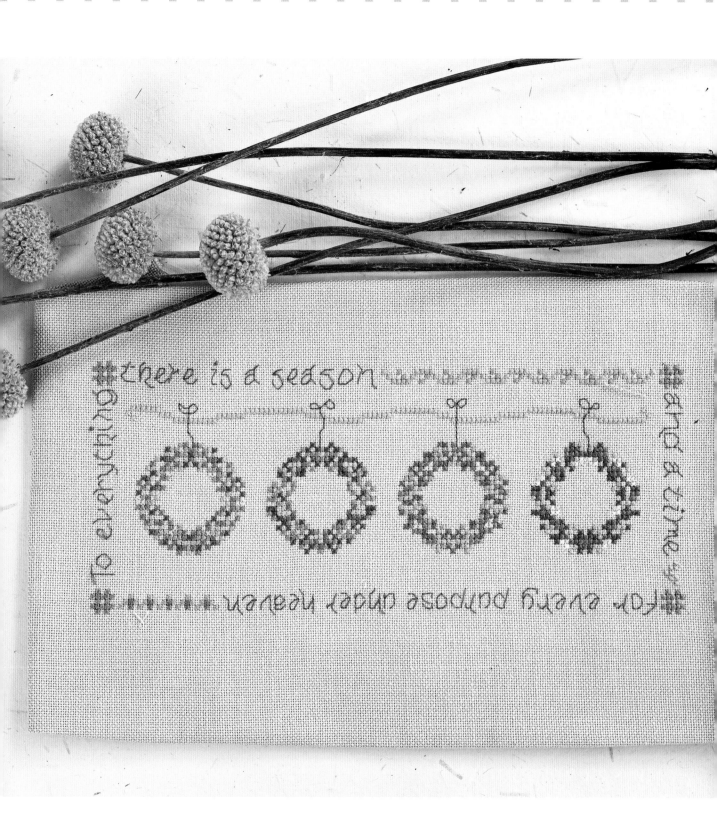

To Everything a Season

This is such a lovely quote from the Bible (which has also been used in folk music and poetry). I think it's meaningful to us all because it reminds us that, just like the seasons in our garden, we, too, go through periods of change, growth, and harvest. This is, to me, one of the most powerful lessons of the earth and one that keeps us grounded in faith and hope, whatever season of the soul we may currently be experiencing.

> **Fabric:** 28-count Waterlily Jobelan by Wichelt (stitched over 2 threads)
> **Stitch count:** 125 wide x 51 high
> **Stitched size:** 9 x 3¾ in. (22.7 x 9.25 cm)

The piece of linen must be at least 3 inches (7.6 cm) larger than the finished size of the stitching, on all sides. This is a good general rule to follow for all projects, although if I think the fabric is particularly prone to fraying (as is the case with many linens), I will cut it a bit larger all around, up to 5 inches (12.7 cm). Fold the fabric in half and count out to begin stitching at a suitable point. For this design, I recommend, again, that you stitch the border and lettering first, before doing the central flower wreaths.

This design has not been finished and is presented as a flat piece; however, there are a number of finishing options, such as a framed piece or decorative pillow. The flower wreaths of the design also lend themselves to being stitched individually, as tiny pillows, cards, or other small decorative pieces.

Floss Used for Full Stitches:

Symbol		Strands	Type	Number	Color
▫	<	2	DMC	153	Violet-VY LT
▪	o	2	DMC	522	Fern Green
▫	>	2	DMC	524	Fern Green-VY LT
▪	c	2	DMC	553	Violet
▫	I	2	DMC	644	Beige Gray-MD
▫	/	2	DMC	676	Old Gold-LT
▫	~	2	DMC	677	Old Gold-VY LT
▪	)	2	DMC	761	Salmon-LT
▪	(	2	DMC	932	Antique Blue-LT
▫	1	2	DMC	3013	Khaki Green-LT
▫	↑	2	DMC	3053	Green Gray
▪	r	2	DMC	3347	Yellow Green-MD
▪	+	2	DMC	3363	Pine Green-MD
▫	∧	2	DMC	3364	Pine Green
▪	v	2	DMC	3712	Salmon-MD
▫	-	2	DMC	3778	Terra Cotta-LT
▫	4	2	DMC	3813	Blue Green-LT
▪	n	2	DMC	3828	Hazelnut Brown
▫	L	2	DMC	3855	Autumn Gold-LT
▪	3	2	DMC	3863	Mocha Beige-MD
▫	·	2	DMC	3865	Winter White

Floss Used for French Knots:

Symbol		Strands	Type	Number	Color
▪	●	1	DMC	640	Beige Gray-VY DK

Floss Used for Back Stitches:

Symbol		Strands	Type	Number	Color
▪	——	1	DMC	640	Beige Gray-VY DK
▪	——	1	DMC	3363	Pine Green-MD

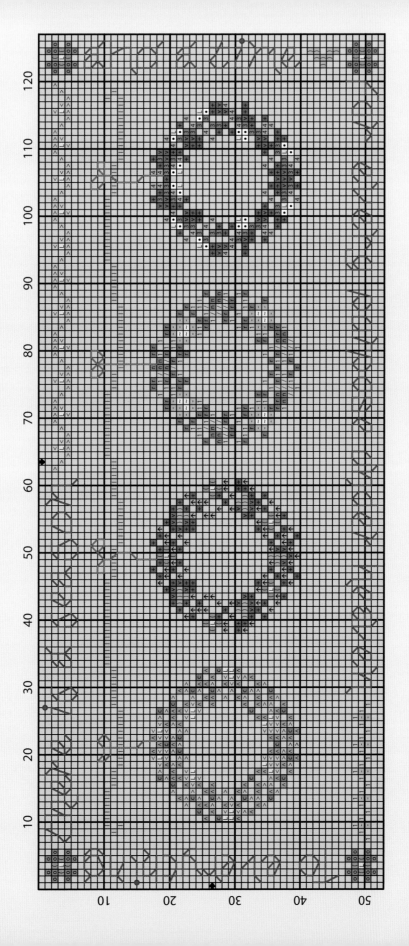

85

"We can never have enough nature."
Henry David Thoreau

Walk Gently . . .

Our earth is the only one we have—she nurtures and sustains us on so many levels—but, sadly, the earth is also under considerable strain these days. We can all play our part in caring for our home, even in simple ways like reducing our use of plastics and recycling wherever practicable. When we walk gently and with love and respect on this earth, we encourage others to do the same and ensure that future generations will also be able to share this gift!

Fabric: 28-count antique white Jobelan by Wichelt (stitched over 2 threads)
Stitch count: 96 wide x 67 high
Stitched size: 6¾ x 5 in. (17.4 x 12.6 cm)

Cut fabric to measure at least 10 inches wide by 9 inches high (25.4 x 22.9 cm). Fold and then count out to start stitching at a suitable point. When stitching is done, wash and press lightly (if necessary).

You will need a purchased oval board, measuring at least 8½ inches wide by 6¼ inches high (21.6 x 15.9 cm). Glue a piece of soft white felt or similar fabric to one side of the board. Trim the stitched piece into an oval shape that is at least 1½ inches (3.8 cm) larger than the board, and then place the piece over the fabric-covered side of the board and fold around to the back, ensuring that the design is centered and straight. Hold in place at the back with double-sided tape; cover the back of the board with another piece of felt or fabric and glue in place. Finally, glue a piece of coordinating satin ribbon right around the oval shape and form into a decorative bow at the top (which you can hold in place with some decorative pins).

Floss Used for Full Stitches:

	Symbol	Strands	Type	Number	Color
	>	2	DMC	152	Shell Pink-MD LT
	v	2	DMC	223	Shell Pink-LT
	r	2	DMC	316	Antique Mauve-MD
	c	2	DMC	522	Fern Green
	-	2	DMC	524	Fern Green-VY LT
	H	2	DMC	642	Beige Gray-DK
	n	2	DMC	676	Old Gold-LT
	((	2	DMC	677	Old Gold-VY LT
	e	2	DMC	729	Old Gold-MD
	o	2	DMC	822	Beige Gray-LT
	/	2	DMC	926	Gray Green-MD
	~	2	DMC	927	Gray Green-LT
	)	2	DMC	3013	Khaki Green-LT
	m	2	DMC	3041	Antique Violet-MD
	¬	2	DMC	3042	Antique Violet-LT
	<	2	DMC	3053	Green Gray
	L	2	DMC	3363	Pine Green-MD
	^	2	DMC	3364	Pine Green
	l	2	DMC	3727	Antique Mauve-LT
	1	2	DMC	3855	Autumn Gold-LT
	+	2	DMC	3863	Mocha Beige-MD

Floss Used for French Knots:

	Symbol	Strands	Type	Number	Color
	●	1	DMC	3863	Mocha Beige-MD

Floss Used for Back Stitches:

	Symbol	Strands	Type	Number	Color
	——	1	DMC	3863	Mocha Beige-MD

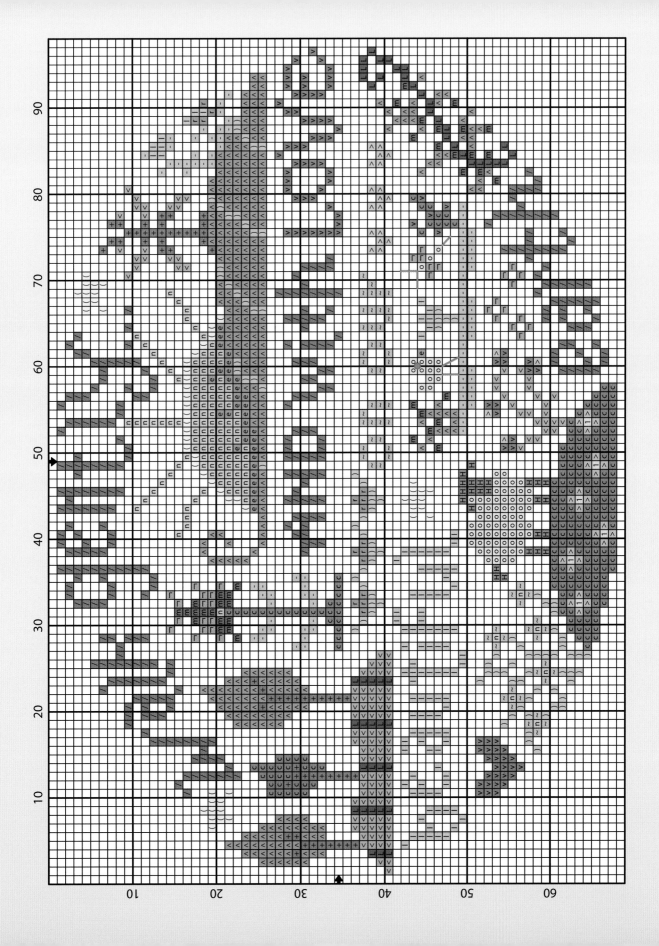

Everything grows
in my mother's garden

seeds of patience

blossoms of hope

flowers of kindness

fruits of understanding

stitched for Catharine

In My Mother's Garden

This is a piece I designed some years ago as a gift for my mom on her birthday. It seemed appropriate to revise the design for this book, which is very largely a tribute to my mother. I think she would be delighted that I have included it here. The piece is done in the style of traditional band samplers, which I have always loved; they are also very satisfying and surprisingly quick to stitch! To make the design more versatile, I have added wording for "sister's" and "friend's" garden to the bottom of the chart.

Fabric: 32-count ivory linen by Wichelt (stitched over 2 threads)
Stitch count: 61 wide x 155 high
Stitched size: 4½ x 9¼ in. (11.7 x 23.5 cm)

Cut fabric to measure at least 9 inches wide and 15 inches high (22.9 x 38.1 cm); fold in half and count out to start stitching at a convenient point—again, the border is a good place to start. When stitching is complete, wash and press lightly (if necessary). Cut a piece of suitable board to measure 5½ x 11 inches (14 x 27.9 cm), and then stretch the stitched piece over the board and glue or lace the fabric in place at the back, ensuring that the design is straight and centered. Glue on a length of ribbon at the top of the piece for hanging, and then cut a piece of fabric/felt to cover the back of the piece.

JACKY PARKER PHOTOGRAPHY/MOMENT VIA GETTY IMAGES

" In search of my mother's garden,
I found my own."

Alice Walker

Floss Used for Full Stitches:

Symbol		Strands	Type	Number	Color
◼	o	2	DMC	223	Shell Pink-LT
◻	I	2	DMC	224	Shell Pink-VY LT
◼	<	2	DMC	502	Blue Green
◼	⋈	2	DMC	640	Beige Gray-VY DK
◻	-	2	DMC	644	Beige Gray-MD
◻	~	2	DMC	677	Old Gold-VY LT
◻	·	2	DMC	822	Beige Gray-LT
◼	n	2	DMC	926	Gray Green-MD
◻	L	2	DMC	927	Gray Green-LT
◻	>	2	DMC	3042	Antique Violet-LT
◻	m	2	DMC	3046	Yellow Beige-MD
◻	)	2	DMC	3047	Yellow Beige-LT
◻	c	2	DMC	3727	Antique Mauve-LT
◻	∧	2	DMC	3813	Blue Green-LT
◼	/	2	DMC	3816	Celadon Green-MD

Floss Used for French Knots:

Symbol		Strands	Type	Number	Color
◼	●	1	DMC	223	Shell Pink-LT
◻	●	1	DMC	224	Shell Pink-VY LT
◼	●	1	DMC	640	Beige Gray-VY DK
◻	●	1	DMC	3042	Antique Violet-LT
◻	●	1	DMC	3046	Yellow Beige-MD

Floss Used for Back Stitches:

Symbol		Strands	Type	Number	Color
◼	▬▬▬	1	DMC	502	Blue Green
◼	▬▬▬	1	DMC	640	Beige Gray-VY DK
◻	▬▬▬	1	DMC	822	Beige Gray-LT
◼	▬▬▬	1	DMC	3816	Celadon Green-MD

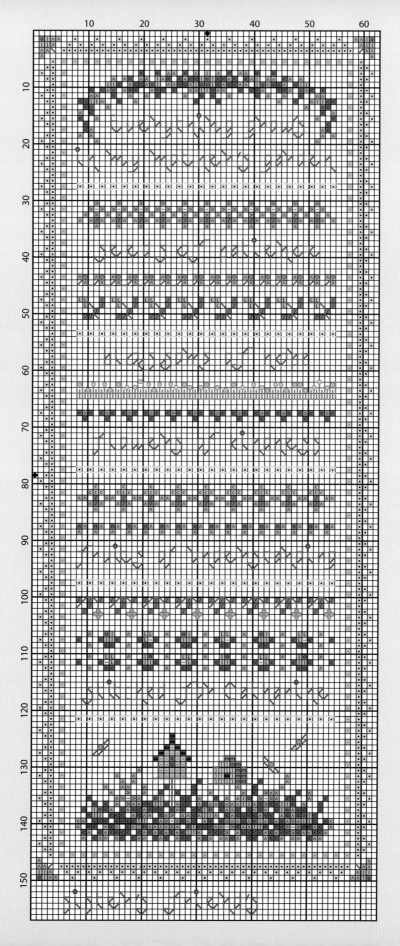

95

Deep Roots Bunny Sampler

A piece for everyone who loves Beatrix Potter—and bunnies! It's also a reminder that we can grow good things to eat in our gardens and nourish ourselves and those we love with the bounty of the earth. This is a quick and simple-to-stitch piece and would make a cute addition to a child's room; if you like, it could be personalized with initials and a date using a simple alphabet like the one on page 105.

Fabric: 32-count antique white Jobelan by Wichelt (stitched over 2 threads)
Stitch count: 63 wide x 63 high
Stitched size: 4½ x 4½ in. (11.4 x 11.4 cm)

Cut your fabric to measure at least 8 inches (20.3 cm) square, and then fold in half and count out to start stitching at a suitable point. When stitching is complete, wash and press lightly (if necessary). This design was finished in a 5½ inch (14 cm) wooden hoop; trim the fabric in a circle that measures about 6½ inches (16.5 cm), and then carefully insert it into the hoop, making sure the design is centered before you tighten the hoop. Add a loop of ribbon for hanging.

Carrot Cupcake Recipe

Bunnies love carrots, as we all know, and this simple carrot cupcake recipe would undoubtedly be as popular with them as it is with us:

Preheat the oven to 350°F. In a large bowl, mix together ½ cup milk, ½ cup vegetable oil, ⅓ cup brown sugar, and 2 eggs. In another bowl, sift together 1 cup cake flour, 1 cup whole wheat flour, 2 teaspoons baking powder, and ½ teaspoon ground cinnamon. Take two juicy carrots, peel and grate them, and then add them to the milk mixture together with ¼ cup raisins. Combine this mixture with the flour mixture and beat until smooth. Line 12 large (or 24 mini) cupcake pans with liners, and then fill ⅔ full with the mixture. Bake for 15–20 minutes, until the cakes are risen and golden brown. Cool on a wire rack. Serve fresh, either plain or topped with a swirl of your favorite cream cheese frosting.

Floss Used for Full Stitches:

	Symbol	Strands	Type	Number	Color
	-	2	DMC	02	Lightest Gray
	·	2	DMC	03	Med Lightest Gray
	^	2	DMC	352	Coral-LT
	>	2	DMC	353	Peach
	(	2	DMC	402	Mahogany-VY LT
	)	2	DMC	437	Tan-LT
	<	2	DMC	676	Old Gold-LT
	~	2	DMC	677	Old Gold-VY LT
	/	2	DMC	738	Tan-VY LT
	+	2	DMC	761	Salmon-LT
	m	2	DMC	3012	Khaki Green-MD
	l	2	DMC	3013	Khaki Green-LT
	v	2	DMC	3347	Yellow Green-MD
	n	2	DMC	3348	Yellow Green-LT
	c	2	DMC	3364	Pine Green
	o	2	DMC	3712	Salmon-MD

Floss Used for French Knots:

	Symbol	Strands	Type	Number	Color
	●	1	DMC	535	Ash Gray-VY LT
	○	1	DMC	677	Old Gold-VY LT
	●	1	DMC	3363	Pine Green-MD

Floss Used for Back Stitches:

	Symbol	Strands	Type	Number	Color
	——	1	DMC	535	Ash Gray-VY LT
	——	1	DMC	3363	Pine Green-MD

"When you have a garden, you have a future.
And when you have a future, you are alive."
Frances Hodgson Burnett

CHARTING AND ALPHABETS TO CREATE YOUR OWN DESIGNS

Adapting existing cross-stitch patterns or creating your own with words or sayings that are particularly meaningful to you is not difficult and is wonderfully rewarding. The designs in this book are such that many of them can be adapted in various ways, starting with the colors used. If you don't like the colors in a particular design, simply swap them out for ones that you prefer. (Just remember to keep the general depth of color in mind—darker shades and paler ones, as needed.)

If you wish to create your own sayings, it is possible to get several charting systems that make this process a breeze. I have used Patternmaker for Cross Stitch (a program by HobbyWare) for many years now and find it very easy and user friendly—but, of course, you may find another favorite.

Alternatively, most of my designs start life in the old-fashioned way, with a pencil, colored pens or markers, an eraser (very important!), and lots of graph paper. First, choose the count of the fabric you are going to use (28-count = 14 stitches to the inch; 32-count = 16 stitches to the inch). Work out how much space you are going to need for your chosen words/saying, and then measure this area out on the graph paper. Use a pencil to lightly sketch the words/quote in this space. Then fill in the blocks with lettering of your choice. You can use any of the ideas given in this book or the additional alphabet charts. Or you can make up your own lettering, as I generally do—there are no rules. Sometimes a word/ saying is centered on the graph, and other times it is randomly placed down or across the piece, as you will see from the different designs in this book.

Do remember that writing in whole stitches is generally done in a paler shade of floss than backstitch lettering, which is done in a single strand of floss and thus needs a darker or more intense color to stand out.

If you wish to change the words/quotes on any of the existing designs in this book, first photocopy the chart, enlarging it if necessary. Then cut a piece of squared/graph paper to cover the existing words, glue it down, and fill in the words of your choice.

Happy stitching and creating!

Floss Used for Full Stitches:

Symbol		Strands	Type	Number	Color
■	▣ o	2	DMC	931	Antique Blue-MD
■	▣ -	2	DMC	932	Antique Blue-LT

Floss Used for French Knots:

Symbol		Strands	Type	Number	Color
■	●	1	DMC	931	Antique Blue-MD

Floss Used for Back Stitches:

Symbol		Strands	Type	Number	Color
■	———	1	DMC	931	Antique Blue-MD

Note:
Fabric varies according to the design being stitched.

ACKNOWLEDGMENTS

I'd also like to include the following short note of thanks:

First, my thanks for Candi Derr and all at Stackpole who took a chance on my first book with them; I appreciate your confidence and support with this, my second book. Also, to my friends who have put up with my endless hours of stitching and complaining about my sore eyes/hands! To the people at Wichelt, especially Amy Wichelt and Mary Prindle, who have supplied me with the fabrics I needed to complete these projects—I could not have done it without you! And to all those who have instilled a love of gardens and growing things in me—most especially the spirit of my late mom—I am grateful and blessed in so many ways by these lessons and love.

VISUAL INDEX

The Secret Garden 3

In Sunshine 8

Herbs of Grace 13

Flowers Are Happy Things 19

Song of the Birds   23

Heart of a Rose   29

Ladybug Cottage   35

Love Is the Honey   39

Cathy's Garden Quilt 45

Earth Is a Garden 49

Sweet Petals 52

Plant Your Garden 57

Where Flowers Bloom . . . 61

Tea in My Garden 65

A Butterfly Blessing 71

How to Be a Sunflower 77

To Everything a Season   83

Walk Gently . . .   87

In My Mother's Garden   91

Deep Roots Bunny Sampler   97

Life is the flower... Love is the Honey